MILITARY JOBS

COUNTERTERRORISM OPERATIVES

What It Takes to Join the Elite

TIM RIPLEY

Cavendish
Square
New York

Published in 2016 by Cavendish Square Publishing, LLC
243 5th Avenue, Suite 136, New York, NY 10016

© 2016 Brown Bear Books Ltd

First Edition

Website: cavendishsq.com

This publication represents the opinions and views of the author based on his or her personal experiences, knowledge, and research. The information in this book serves as a general guide only. the author and publisher have used their best efforts in preparing this book and disclaim liability rising directly or indirectly from the use and application of this book.

CPSIA Compliance Information: Batch #WS15CSQ

Library of Congress Cataloging-in-Publication Data

Ripley, Tim.
Counterterrorism operatives : what it takes to join the elite / Tim Ripley.
pages cm. — (Military jobs)
Includes bibliographical references and index.
ISBN 978-1-50260-514-6 (hardcover) ISBN 978-1-50260-515-3 (ebook)
1. Special forces (Military science)—United States. 2. Special forces (Military science)—United States—Vocational guidance. 3. Terrorism—Prevention—United States. 4. Special operations (Military science)—United States. I. Title.

UA34.S64R57 2016
363.325'1702373—dc23

2014049221

For Brown Bear Books Ltd:
Editorial Director: Lindsey Lowe
Managing Editor: Tim Cooke
Children's Publisher: Anne O'Daly
Design Manager: Keith Davis
Designer: Lynne Lennon
Picture Manager: Sophie Mortimer

Picture Credits:
T=Top, C=Center, B=Bottom, L=Left, R=Right

Front Cover: U.S. Department of Defense
All images U.S. Department of Defense except: Alamy: Everett Collection Historical 45; Getty Images: Asif Hassan 44, CNN 39, Oleg Nikishin 39.
Artistic Effects: Shutterstock

Brown Bear Books has made every attempt to contact the copyright holder.
If you have any information please contact licensing@brownbearbooks.co.uk.

We believe the extracts included in this book to be material in the public domain.
Anyone having any further information should contact licensing@brownbearbooks.co.uk.

Manufactured in the United States of America

CONTENTS

INTRODUCTION

Modern conflicts rarely involve battles against enemy forces. Instead, the greatest threat to US forces comes from terrorist groups who use irregular tactics such as assassination, kidnap, and booby traps.

Every member of the US military is involved in some way in the fight against terrorism. The military and law enforcement agencies lead the defense against terror attacks. Soldiers and special Female Engagement Teams (FETs) in war zones try to prevent people from becoming terrorists.

The military campaign is spearheaded by different branches of US Special Forces: the Army Green Berets and Rangers, and the Navy SEALs (Sea, Air, and Land teams). One specialist counterterrorism unit is the Army's Delta Force. Most details about the unit's activities are kept secret. Another shadowy unit is SEAL Team 6. They became famous after killing terrorist leader Osama bin Laden in 2011. This book mainly concentrates on these two units, whose names strike fear into the hearts of terrorists everywhere.

 An assault team of US Army Rangers keeps its weapons ready as its helicopter comes in to land.

►► HISTORY

For US forces, the fight against terrorist groups began during the war in Vietnam (1963–1975). Viet Cong terrorists hiding among the South Vietnamese population launched attacks on US forces.

The Viet Cong (VC) supported communist North Vietnam. They lived in underground tunnels and launched surprise attacks.

US Army Green Berets pose with South Vietnamese soldiers. They helped them to hunt Viet Cong guerrillas.

Green Berets

America used special forces to try to defeat the Viet Cong. Army special forces, called the Green Berets, trained local Vietnamese people to help them find enemy guerrillas. They also

 In the 1980s the emphasis of counterterrorism switched to operations in Central America.

provided services such as medical care to villagers, in order to win their support.

SEALs and Rangers

The Navy SEALs fought for the first time in Vietnam. They went into hostile territory to ambush enemy units and rescue US prisoners. Meanwhile, Army Rangers carried out long-range patrols behind enemy lines to gather essential intelligence. The Special Forces developed their counterterrorism role after the Vietnam War. When the attacks of September 11, 2001, struck the United States, Special Forces helped with the US response, called the "War on Terror."

IN ACTION

The Vietnam War showed how useful Special Forces could be. They became a more important part of military operations. In the 1980s, special forces were in action in Central America and Africa. After the terrorist attacks of 9/11, Special Forces led US operations in Afghanistan and Iraq.

⟩⟩ WHAT IT TAKES

The Special Forces are the elite of the US military. They are among the best trained troops in the world. All candidates have to possess above average intelligence, physical fitness, and initiative.

The Special Forces members involved in counterterrorism operations usually operate in small groups. They need to be self-sufficient, because there is no support organization while they are on a mission. They also have to be able to adapt to the changing circumstances of a mission without

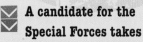 **A candidate for the Special Forces takes on an assault course.**

waiting for orders, so they are expected to have a high degree of initiative.

The Elite of the Elite

Couterterrorist operations can involve long periods in hostile territory. Candidates have to be able to cope with high levels of stress. They also need to have the physical fitness to be able to go without sleep or food, but still make dependable decisions. Because communications are so important, candidates often speak more than one foreign language.

 Special Forces trainees hold out their rifles in an exercise designed to measure their physical and mental resilience and stamina.

IN ACTION

Being a counterterrorism operative is not an official job in the military. Counterterrorism duties are just one of the tasks facing all members of the Special Forces. Other tasks include unconventional warfare, such as sabotage; training foreign soldiers or guerrilla groups in other countries; and carrying out secret reconnaissance.

▶▶ INDIVIDUAL SELECTION

Candidates for America's elite counterterrorist units—Delta Force and their US Navy counterparts in SEAL Team 6—face demanding selection regimes. Fewer than 10 percent of applicants get through.

The selection process not only pushes potential counterterrorism operatives to their physical limits. It also assesses whether they have the mental resilience that will enable them to keep fighting in extreme situations.

The Best Recruits

Delta Force (the 1st Special Operations Detachment–Delta) and SEAL Team 6 (the US Naval Special Warfare Development Group, or NSWDG) only recruit from

▶▶ The strain of a log exercise shows in the face of an Army Special Forces candidate.

 Candidates pause during an exercise carrying ammunition boxes on a long hike.

serving members of the US military. All candidates need to have shown outstanding skills in their previous units.

Physical Tests

Applicants first undergo a grueling series of physical tests. These start with push-ups and sit-ups but increase in intensity to include exercises moving heavy logs and undertaking 40-mile (64 km) navigation exercises in full combat

gear. If they pass the physical tests, applicants are screened to assess if they are psychologically suitable for counterterrorism work.

EYEWITNESS

"To get through the challenges and hardships of [selection] you have to have the desire to succeed and that comes from your heart. If you have any doubts there is a good chance you'll lose heart and you will quit."

—Ed Bugarin, former Delta Force operator

►► DELTA FORCE BASIC TRAINING

Successful recruits to Delta Force go straight to the Operator Training Course, or OTC. The world's leading counterterrorism course prepares them to fight in all types of terrain and in complex situations.

 A Delta Force operator keeps watch as his colleagues question a "civilian" during a hostage-rescue exercise.

At the heart of the six-month OTC is marksmanship training. Close-quarter battle training prepares applicants to use their weapons in confined spaces, against moving and stationary targets.

▷▷▷ Members of Delta Force cover one another as they leave a building during a simulated hostage rescue.

The course moves on to demolition and obstacle breaching. Recruits learn how to use explosives and weapons to break into fortified houses and other structures.

Another part of the course covers advanced intelligence gathering. This teaches recruits how to carry out surveillance on terrorists to find out about their positions, equipment, and weaknesses.

The Killing House

At the end of the OTC, applicants test all their skills in simulated hostage rescue missions carried out in a facility known as the "killing house." They also practice attacks on commercial airliners, trains, or tower blocks, supported by helicopters and other aircraft.

EYEWITNESS

"I've seen many operators from different units who beat their chest and think they're special. These are the guys I shun. An operator isn't special. Rather he/she is unique."

—Ed Bugarin, former Delta Force operator

>> SEAL TRAINING

Counterterrorist operations at sea are the job of SEAL Team 6. Recruits are already Navy SEALs skilled at underwater demolition, using small boats, and making landings on enemy beaches.

Training for SEAL Team 6 takes these skills to a higher level. Operatives are taught how to carry out hostage rescue and other missions in a wide range of situations.

 SEALs practice rapid target identification, which is essential in close-range urban fighting.

Seal Team 6 recruits practice rescuing civilians or prisoners of war held by terrorists. They simulate attacks on cruise liners, oil tankers, offshore drilling platforms, or fishing boats.

Mock Battles

This training revolves around intense close-quarter battle drills. The hopeful SEAL Team 6 recruits carry out repeated simulated assaults during mock battles. Teams are drilled to make rapid entry into a location and then neutralize any terrorists before attempting to release any hostages.

 Candidates for SEAL Basic Underwater Demolition (BUD/S) training do exercises on a beach. Physical training is constant for all Special Forces operators.

EYEWITNESS

"We all knew there was just one way to improve our odds for survival: train, train, train. Sometimes, if your training is properly intense it will kill you. More often—much, much more often—it will save your life."

—Richard Marcinko, founder, SEAL Team 6

►► STRIKE TRAINING

The primary mission of Delta Force and SEAL Team 6 is to find and neutralize hostile terrorist groups anywhere in the world. Often, the best way to do this is to strike directly at the terrorists' home base.

These strike missions often mean raids deep inside hostile territory. Counterterrorism operatives spend months preparing for these demanding missions. They use close reconnaissance to find the

 Special Forces return from a live fire small-arms exercise.

location of individual terrorists, as well as their weapons and defensive positions. Drones and surveillance satellites help build up a picture of the enemy, but to plan the final stages of an assault needs "eyes on target." This means operatives need to get into position so they can study the location for themselves.

Assault Operations

Training for assault operations is methodical. Operatives develop their skills in weapons handling, forced entry techniques, target recognition, and extraction procedures. In a series of assault exercises, operators "take down" a range of targets in simulated attacks. Video cameras record the exercises so instructors can debrief the troops.

IN ACTION

Counterterrorism operatives often have to fight in urban locations. The focus of much of their training is on close quarters battle (CQB) operations. They fight in small groups, often in confined locations. Operatives must become expert at quickly identifying terrorists from innocent civilians as they clear streets and buildings.

▷▷▷ **SEAL recruits prepare to enter a building during close-quarter battle training.**

▶▶ HOSTAGE RESCUE TRAINING

One of the most difficult counterterrorism tasks is the rescue of hostages held by terror groups. Counterterrorism operatives have to learn highly specialized tactics and procedures.

 Counterterrorism operatives practice stopping a car to rescue a hostage.

Operatives learn how to build up accurate intelligence about a hostage situation. They are trained in the use of hidden cameras, listening

devices, surveillance sensors, and night-vision glasses in order to find out the relative positions of the hostages and their captors.

 US Marines take on the roles of hostages and kidnapper during a rescue exercise.

Into Danger

In live-ammunition exercises, operatives learn to use explosives or battering rams to open doors and windows. They throw stun grenades to disorient the terrorists. Rescue teams learn to move through dark buildings and kill any terrorists they find. They are taught to tell terrorists and hostages apart so they avoid accidental injuries.

EYEWITNESS

"Delta Force was, and is, known for its superb planning process, its scientific approach to assaults, and its extraordinary marksmanship and physical training. It is equal or superior to any other counter-terror force in the world."

—Danny Coulson, founder, FBI Hostage Rescue Team

▷▷ TARGET SURVEILLANCE

Reliable intelligence gathering is at the heart of effective counterterrorism operations. Operatives use observation tactics to set up 24/7 surveillance of suspected terrorist targets.

As counterterrorist forces prepare for an assault, they need still and video imagery of the target from all angles. For this, a covert observation-post team is put in position close to the target for days or weeks ahead of an operation. They must build up a "pattern of life" for both the terrorists and any civilians nearby.

▷▷ **A Navy SEAL uses a camera with a special lens to photograph an enemy position.**

<<< A Special Forces captain studies the landscape of Georgia, in eastern Europe, through binoculars during an exercise with officers from the Georgian army.

This process enables the assault commander to determine the terrorists' routine to work out the best timing of any attack.

Overhead Cameras

During the assault, commanders keep an eye on progress using drones. The information they gather allows them to warn their troops of enemy movements or to call for airborne fire support to neutralize threats.

EYEWITNESS

"We gather intelligence from behind enemy lines. We watch life unfold in an area where no one knows we exist. We need that 'quiet professional' who we know is doing the right thing regardless of the situation."

—Darren James, Long Range Surveillance Unit

 # RAIDS

Delta Force and SEAL Team 6—and other special forces, like the Army Rangers—keep teams on alert to launch raids anywhere in the world in response to terrorist threats. A decision to launch a raid is taken at the highest levels of government.

A raid might be ordered to capture a terrorist leader dead or alive. Other raids might be ordered to recover terrorist intelligence material, such as documents or computers, for analysis.

Always Ready

Counterterrorism assault forces are kept on alert for these types of missions at bases both within the United States and in forward locations close to regions where terrorist threat levels are high.

Special Forces from the Army Rangers stage a raid in a simulated urban setting.

▶▶ Operatives use pistols to provide cover for one another as they search a terrorist hideout.

Insertion Phase

The insertion phase is the key to a successful operation. Success often relies on the element of surprise. Although helicopters can provide rapid movement to the target, the noise of their rotors can sometimes alert terrorists. Instead, operatives often make long forced marches at night. They arrive silently, and can take terrorists by surprise.

After an assault is over and the mission objectives have been achieved, a rapid extraction of the assault force is needed. Helicopters bring them out of enemy territory, along with any captured terrorists and intelligence material that has been gathered.

EYEWITNESS

"It's their ability to learn, adapt, and react without overreacting or going off on a tangent or having preconceived ideas that makes the Special Forces so useful."

—**Robert Young Pelton, war reporter, Aghanistan, 2003**

▶▶ HOSTAGE RESCUE MISSIONS

Hostage rescue is so risky that it is only attempted when there is no alternative. The Joint Special Operations Command (JSOC) sends in a team from Delta Force or SEAL Team 6.

During an exercise, a member of an assault team covers terrorists pulled from a car.

Hostage rescue operations are complex. They involve intelligence gathering, surveillance, transportation, assault, and diversion and deception activities. These operations all have to be synchronized in order to take the terrorists by surprise and so safely free the hostages. Both Delta Force and SEAL Team 6 have dedicated hostage rescue teams on permanent alert to move into action at a few hours' notice.

 US Black Hawk helicopters drop rescue teams as close to a hostage location as possible.

Striking Fast

When called into action, these units move quickly to the scene to prepare a strike. At the same time, intelligence work begins to determine who is holding the hostages and where. Getting the assault team into position without being detected is often the most difficult part of a rescue. They use civilian vehicles to blend into the local background and confuse the hostage takers.

Rescue missions often take place in countries hostile to the United States. Aircraft, warships, and attack helicopters provide a defensive shield as the assault troops bring the hostages to safety.

EYEWITNESS

"We were trained to do one job: kill terrorists and rescue hostages, and do it better than anybody in the world."

—Richard Marcinko, founder, SEAL Team 6

▶▶ WORKING WITH LOCAL FORCES

Terrorist groups often hide among civilian populations, where it is very difficult to identify them. US counterterrorism operatives rely on their local allies for help. They also train local forces to take on terrorists themselves.

All US Special Forces are experts at working with local allies and are excellent communicators. Counterterrorism operatives often work under cover with foreign intelligence agencies and military forces to gather information. If terrorists are based in remote locations, operatives recruit local tribes or militias to provide protection.

▶▶ **Afghan police trained by US Special Forces prepare to carry out a raid.**

Recruiting Support

US counterterrorism operatives use diplomatic skills to recruit locals as sources of information. They live with local communities and learn to understand them, so they can persuade tribes to help act against the terrorists.

Local custom in Afghanistan prevents male soldiers speaking to Afghan women. The US Marines and Army have special Female Engagement Teams (FETs). These female soldiers carry out patrols and interact with local people.

 Members of a US Marine FET enter a village leader's compound in Helmand province, Afghanistan.

EYEWITNESS

"These guys deal on a social level, they live with these people. They have to deal with women and children and tribal rivalries and all kinds of complex social issues."

—Robert Young Pelton, war reporter, Aghanistan, 2003

UNDERWATER OPERATIONS

At sea, the threat comes from modern-day pirates as well as terrorists. Targets such as merchant ships, offshore oil platforms, harbors, bridges, and other coastal facilities are all vulnerable to attack.

Dealing with terrorists or pirates at sea calls for specialist tactics and equipment. SEAL Team 6 is trained to face this kind of specialized threat. The unit is also trained in underwater reconnaissance. It uses scuba diving gear to approach a hostile terrorist location by sea and gathers information without ever leaving the water. Operatives are trained in sign language so they can communicate underwater.

A SEAL leaves the water with his pistol at the ready. All SEAL weapons are fully waterproof.

28

Attacking at Sea

If terrorists hold a position at sea, such as a boat or oil platform, it is difficult to launch a surprise attack. Anyone approaching is easy to spot across the open water.

SEAL assault teams are dropped close to the target by submarine. They are also trained to parachute into the sea from an airplane or helicopter. They use scuba gear or a mini submarine called a SEAL Delivery Vehicle (SDV) to get into position for an assault. This allows them to achieve surprise.

 SEAL combat swimmers operate in pairs. This menas that they can cover one another underwater.

EYEWITNESS

"A submerged reconnaissance is the most complex mission I ever ran as a SEAL officer. All communication would be in sign language. Every man had to know not only his own assignment but everyone else's so he could take over any role if we had casualties."

—Robert A. Gormly, former US Navy SEAL

>> SMALL ARMS

Elite counterterrorism operatives in the US Special Forces rely on being better armed than the enemy. For close-range fighting on the ground, they carry the world's best small arms and automatic weapons.

A Navy SEAL fires an MP5 submachine gun. It has a short barrel to make it easier to carry and use.

One key task is to provide suppressing fire, which is constant gunfire that keeps the enemy pinned down and unable to move. For this, Delta Force and SEAL Team 6 usually use the Colt M4 carbine. The Heckler & Koch MP7 machine pistol is also a popular weapon, because it is reliable at close range. Operatives also use the 416 assault rifle, which provides heavier firepower.

 Counterterrorism operatives practice firing M9A1 Beretta pistols from a warship at sea.

For long-range firepower, the 0.50mm caliber Browning M82A1 Objective Sniper Weapon (OSW) is popular. It has the power to smash through even the toughest body armor. It is also effective at destroying matériel, such as trucks or airplanes.

Hand Guns

All counterterrorism operatives carry pistols. The small arms give them tactical options when fighting in confined spaces, such as buildings or airliners, where an assault weapon is too cumbersome or too powerful to be used safely. Pistols are also backups in case an operative's assault weapon malfunctions in action.

IN ACTION

Unlike other soldiers, Special Forces operatives often fit silencers to their weapons. This confuses opponents by concealing their firing positions. They also often have their small arms modified to their personal preferences, including changing hand grips and weapon stocks.

UNIFORMS
AND PERSONAL EQUIPMENT

Elite counterterrorism operatives do not have standard uniforms or haircuts. They simply have to be equipped to face any type of mission. Their basic rule is "Bring what you think you need."

In addition to firearms, operatives also carry hand grenades and fixed-blade knives. Although counterterrorism operatives do not have to wear uniforms on base, they usually go into action wearing battledress. They wear a camouflage pattern suited to the environment, such as the desert or the jungle. Their advanced helmets are made from lightweight Kevlar that protects them against shrapnel and bullets. The helmets also

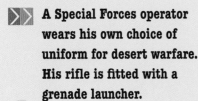
A Special Forces operator wears his own choice of uniform for desert warfare. His rifle is fitted with a grenade launcher.

have mounts for cameras. Some operatives wear thin armor inside their battledress for protection. Others choose not to because the armor plates make it more awkward to move.

Traveling Light

Operatives carry their load in large pockets and in a single chest rig. This is a harness with shoulder straps and a belt with pouches. Operatives cram it with ammunition magazines, radios and batteries, bolt cutters, and other tools, lights, and tourniquets in case they are wounded.

 Counterterrorism operatives carry full loads of equipment in their pockets and chest webbing as they fly into action.

IN ACTION

The special kit required by US counterterrorism units has been in the forefront of the development of new lightweight materials. These plastics and other compounds have dramatically reduced the weight of body armor and ballistic helmets while retaining their protection levels.

▶▶ SURVEILLANCE AND COMMUNICATIONS

Being able to monitor terrorist activity secretly, in all weather, and at night is at the heart of US counterterrorism tactics.

Thermal-imaging cameras and night-vision goggles are standard issue. Thermal imagers allow operatives to monitor enemy troops at long distance. They pick up body heat, so they not only reveal individuals at night, but they also detect "hot spots" in woods or buildings that indicate where terrorists might be hiding.

A Special Forces operator uses night-vision goggles as he uses an antenna to establish radio communication at night.

Thermal imagers are available as sights that operators can fit to their weapons. Stand-alone devices with telephoto lenses are also used by surveillance detachments.

Seeing at Night

Night-vision goggles (NVG) use image-intensifying technology. This uses light from the moon and sources such as distant houses to illuminate the darkness. Operatives wear helmet-mounted NVGs to help them move toward their objectives at night.

 Establishing a secure radio connection is a priority on a mission in hostile territory.

IN ACTION

Counterterrorism operatives use encrypted radios both to talk to their teams and to call in air and fire support. Broadband Internet technology also gives operators in remote locations access to intelligence and video imagery from drones, which is sent directly to their laptops.

▶▶ HOSTAGE RESCUE EQUIPMENT

Hostage rescue depends on intelligence. Mini-drones fly silently overhead to gather information on terrorist-held buildings and vehicles. Directional microphones and fish-eye cameras can be inserted through walls and windows to locate hostages.

Marksmen take aim as an operative prepares to use a ram to break down a door during an exercise.

O nce intelligence has been gathered and the hostages located, the assault team has to gain entry into the building or vehicle. This is often the critical moment in a rescue. To achieve surprise the assault team usually uses

◀◀ Operators use metal shields for protection during a nighttime exercise in hostage rescue.

explosives to blast an entry hole in a wall. To gain entry, they have portable ladders, climbing ropes, and hooks so they can climb up the sides of buildings, onto the fuselages of airplanes, or up the sides of ships.

Special Grenades

As the assault team enters the hole they have made, they use smoke or dazzling grenades to further confuse the terrorists. These explosives and grenades are designed to be less powerful than grenades used in combat, so that they do not cause unintentional injuries to the hostages.

EYEWITNESS

"There's risk, but look at the risk I was in. I was going to be dead for sure, 100 percent. So it's better odds with them coming in to try and help you out. Because otherwise you have no chance."

—Roy Hallums, rescued hostage, Iraq, 2004

⫸ FORT BATTLE IN
MAZAR-E-SHARIF

At the height of the war in Afghanistan in November 2001, US and British Special Forces found themselves locked in a deadly battle in the Qala-e-Jhangí fort.

US Special Forces take cover behind the wall of the fort during the counterattack against the terrorists.

Some 500 Taliban and al-Qaeda terrorists were being held by Afghans allied to the United States in the old fort outside the city of Mazar-e-Sharif. A small team of Special Forces and Central Intelligence Agency (CIA) operatives were in the fort interrogating prisoners to gain

US Special Forces consult with a local ally during the battle.

intelligence on the location of the al-Qaeda chief Osama bin Laden and his close associates.

Prison Break

On November 28, the prisoners suddenly launched a mass uprising using weapons they had concealed in the fort. One CIA agent was killed and the other Special Forces fled. Counterterrorism operatives outside the fort called in air strikes. US operatives then led an assault, aided by local fighters. They cleared the fort, room by room. The last terrorists had hidden in the cellars. The US operatives flooded the building to flush them out.

EYEWITNESS

"At Mazar-e-Sharif, Major Mark Mitchell demonstrated why courage is one of the four values that in special operations is nonnegotiable. He willingly led an attack in the face of overwhelming odds."

—General Bryan Brown, awarding Mitchell the Distinguished Service Cross

⟫ RESCUING PRISONERS

In March 2003, soon after the invasion of Iraq, a US Army convoy was ambushed in the back streets of the city of Nasiriyah. Six Americans were captured, including Private Jessica Lynch.

US prisoner of war Shoshana Johnson is rescued in Iraq in 2003.

Joint Special Operations Task Force 21, which included a Delta Force rescue team, was given the mission of finding and recovering the prisoners.

 US Marines fly Iraqi allies to safety in a helicopter after rescuing them from captivity.

Hospital Rescue

CIA operatives learned that Private Lynch had been wounded and was in the hospital. They provided a video of the hospital, which Delta Force used to plan a rescue. MH-53 Pave Low helicopters delivered the rescue team, while US Marines staged a diversion to distract Iraqi fighters in the city. The Delta Force team rushed into the hospital and recovered Lynch. A few weeks later, they also recovered the other POWs when their Iraqi guards fled during the final days of the invasion.

EYEWITNESS

"I was in that hospital hurting. I wanted out of there. It didn't matter to me if they would have came in skirts and blank guns. They're the ones that came in to rescue me. Those are my heroes. I'm so thankful that they did what they did. They risked their lives."

—Private Jessica Lynch

▶▶ SAVING CAPTAIN PHILLIPS

On April 10, 2009, the US merchant vessel *Maersk Alabama* was hijacked by pirates off the coast of Somalia in the Indian Ocean. Captain Richard Phillips and his crew were taken captive.

The US Navy was ordered to rescue the crew. As two warships sailed into view, three pirates tried to escape in one of the *Maersk Alabama*'s lifeboats. They took Captain Phillips as a hostage.

Members of SEAL Team 6 were parachuted into the Indian Ocean with their specialist equipment. They were transferred by small boat to one of the US warships, out of sight of the pirates.

▶▶ A satellite image shows one of the US warships shadowing the *Maersk Alabama*.

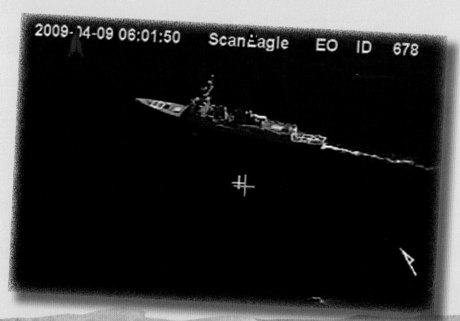

2009-04-09 06:01:50   ScanEagle   EO ID 678

 A US Navy vessel (right) comes alongside the lifeboat after the stand-off was ended by the quick thinking of the SEAL sniper team.

Standoff at Sea

As the warships blocked the escape route of the lifeboat, negotiations began with the pirates for the release of the crew and the ship. A standoff developed that lasted for three days. All that time, SEAL Team 6 snipers were posted on the decks of the warships. They kept their rifles trained on the lifeboat. They kept a close watch on the pirates through telescopic sights, coordinating their actions by radio.

The standoff reached a deadly conclusion. The snipers reported that the pirates were threatening Phillips with an AK-47 rifle. Three SEAL snipers fired simultaneously. Even though they were shooting from a floating ship at long range, they killed all three of the pirates with just three shots. Captain Phillips was rescued unharmed.

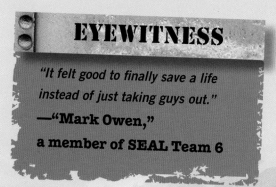

EYEWITNESS

"It felt good to finally save a life instead of just taking guys out."
—"Mark Owen," a member of SEAL Team 6

▶▶ BIN LADEN RAID

After the attacks of September 11 in 2001, US intelligence hunted for Osama bin Laden, the leader of al-Qaeda. After years of work, the CIA tracked him down to a compound in Abbottabad, Pakistan.

SEAL Team 6 was given the mission to assault the walled compound and kill bin Laden. The operation was codenamed Neptune Spear.

Under cover of darkness on May 2, 2011, two UH-60 Black Hawk helicopters approached the compound to deliver the assault team. As it came in to land, one helicopter suffered

▶▶ A Pakistani soldier guards the compound the day after the raid. US authorities did not warn the Pakistani government about the raid.

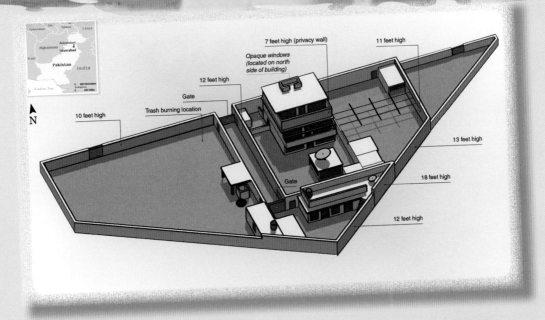

7 feet high (privacy wall)

11 feet high

Opaque windows
(located on north
side of building)

12 feet high

Gate

13 feet high

Trash burning location

10 feet high

18 feet high

N

Gate

12 feet high

a malfunction and crashed. The assault team was uninjured and emerged from the wreckage to begin their attack. They used explosives to blow holes in the high wall and gates to gain entry to the compound.

 This map of the compound was used during planning for the raid.

Death of a Terrorist

The SEALs faced enemy fire as they crossed the compound and entered the house. They cleared the building room by room, killing four people as they moved to the upper stories. Eventually, bin Laden was located and shot dead.

The SEALs removed bin Laden's body, together with computers and other intelligence information. They were on the way back to base by helicopter before Pakistani security forces even arrived.

EYEWITNESS

"The mission was a team effort, from the intelligence analysts who found Osama bin Laden to the helicopter pilots who flew us to Abbottabad to the men who assaulted the compound."

—"Mark Owen,"
a member of SEAL Team 6

GLOSSARY

allies States who formally agree to cooperate to achieve a military purpose.

assets Useful or valuable people working for an agency or unit.

compound A building or group of buildings that is enclosed by a wall.

drones Remote-controlled, unpiloted aerial vehicles.

encrypted Converted into a code for secrecy.

guerrillas Independent fighters who use unconventional tactics, such as boody traps or ambushes.

hostage A person seized and held to force someone else to pay money or fulfill some other condition to ensure his or her release.

insurgents Rebels fighting against a government or an invasion force.

intelligence Information about the enemy that has military value.

Kevlar A very strong synthetic fiber.

matériel A special term used to describe military materials and equipment.

militias Military forces raised from civilians to fight alongside an army in times of emergency.

morale The confidence a person or a group has in their success.

negotiations Discussions aimed at reaching an agreement.

neutralize A small gun designed to be held in one hand.

POW An abbreviation for prisoner of war, an enemy combatant captured during a conflict.

reconnaissance Observation of an enemy's position.

shrapnel Fragments of metal thrown out by an explosion.

sniper A skilled marksman who fires at specific targets from a hidden position.

standoff A dispute between two sides in which there is no progress.

supporting fire Weapons fire that pins the enemy in place in order to prevent them taking action.

surveillance Close observation of the enemy.

terrorist A person who uses acts of violence in order to achieve a political purpose.

tourniquets Bandages used in a medical emergency to prevent blood getting to the lower arm or leg.

FURTHER INFORMATION

BOOKS

Alvarez, Carlos. *Army Delta Force.* Torque Books. Minneapolis, MN: Bellwether Media, 2009.

Cooke, Tim. U.S. *Navy SEALS.* Ultimate Special Forces. New York: PowerKids Press, 2013.

Grinapol, Corinne. *Careers on Antiterrorism and Counterterrorism Task Forces.* Extreme Law Enforcement. New York: Rosen Publishing Group, 2014.

Lusted, Marcia Amidon. *Army Delta Force: Elite Operations.* Military Special Ops. Minneapolis, MN: Lerner Publishing Group, 2013.

Person, Stephen. *Navy SEAL Team Six in Action.* Special Ops II. New York: Bearport Publishing, 2013.

Wasdin, Howard E. *I Am a SEAL Team Six Warrior.* St Louis, MO: Turtleback Books, 2012.

WEBSITES

www.americanspecialops.com/delta-force/selection
Selection requirements for recruits who want to join Delta Force.

www.navy.com/careers/special-operations/seals
US Navy pages about becoming a Navy SEAL.

www.sealswcc.com/seal-default.html
Introduction to the Navy SEALs and their operations.

www.shmoop.com/careers/delta-force/typical-day.html
Shmoop.com guide to life as a Delta Force operator.

Publisher's note to educators and parents: Our editors have carefully reviewed these websites to ensure that they are suitable for students. Many websites change frequently, however, and we cannot guarantee that a site's future contents will continue to meet our high standards of quality and educational value. Be advised that students should be closely supervised whenever they access the Internet.

INDEX